J. M. Barrie

Condensed and Adapted by
WENDI LOWERY

Illustrated by
GREG BECKER

Cover Illustrated by
PATRICK WHELAN

bendon

The Junior Classics have been
adapted and illustrated with care and thought
to introduce you to a world of famous authors, characters, ideas,
and great stories that have been loved for generations.

Editor — Kathryn Knight
Creative Director — Gina Rhodes Haynes
And the entire classics project team
of Bendon Publishing

PETER PAN

Ashland, Ohio 44805 • 1-888-5-BENDON
bendonpub.com

Printed in the United States of America

FOREWORD

A note to the reader—

A classic story rests in your hands. The characters are famous. The tale is timeless.

This Junior Classic edition of *Peter Pan* has been carefully condensed and adapted from the original version (which you really *must* read when you're ready for every detail). We kept the well-known phrases for you. We kept J. M. Barrie's style. And we kept the important imagery and heart of the tale.

Literature is terrific fun! It encourages you to think. It helps you dream. It is full of heroes and villains, suspense and humor, adventure and wonder, and new ideas. It introduces you to writers who reach out across time to say: "Do you want to hear a story I wrote?"

Curl up and enjoy.

CONTENTS

CHARACTERS

THE DARLING HOUSEHOLD

MR. AND MRS. DARLING — a proper British couple, they live at Number 14

WENDY DARLING — the oldest child

JOHN DARLING — the middle child

MICHAEL DARLING — the youngest child

NANA — a Newfoundland dog who looks after the Darling children

LIZA — the housekeeper

PETER PAN — a boy from Neverland who never grows up

TINKER BELL — a rather naughty fairy

THE LOST BOYS — Peter's group of boys

TOOTLES — the unlucky one

NIBS — joyful and carefree

SLIGHTLY — a bit plump, a whistle-maker

CURLY — often in trouble

THE TWINS — they count as two, they answer as one

* * * * * * CHARACTERS * * * * * *

THE PIRATES — fierce villains of Neverland

CAPTAIN JAMES HOOK — hates Peter and fears the crocodile (and is missing his right hand)

SMEE — Hook's "right-hand" man (since Hook is missing one)

HOOK'S CREW

CECCO, BILL JUKES, COOKSON, STARKEY, SKYLIGHTS, ALF MASON, NOODLER

LONG TOM — the cannon, the big gun

PICCANINNY INDIANS — the native tribe

GREAT BIG LITTLE PANTHER — a noble brave

PRINCESS TIGER LILY — a proud and beautiful Indian princess

THE CROCODILE — the *tick-tocking* croc that swallowed a clock

Peter Pan

CHAPTER ONE

Peter Breaks Through

All children, except one, grow up. They soon know that they will grow up, and the way Wendy knew was this. One day when she was two years old she was playing in a garden, and she plucked another flower and ran with it to her mother. I suppose she must have looked rather delightful, for Mrs. Darling put her hand to her heart and cried, "Oh, why can't you remain like this forever?" This was all that passed between them on the subject, but it was then that Wendy knew she would certainly grow up.

Of course they lived at Number 14, and, until Wendy came, her mother was the *only* one for

Mr. Darling. The arrival of baby Wendy was such a happy event that John and Michael soon followed. Mr. and Mrs. Darling were pleased as punch with their little family.

Mrs. Darling loved to have everything just right, so of course they had a nurse. Since they were poor (as the children *did* drink quite a bit of milk, you see), this nurse was a prim Newfoundland dog, called Nana. She had belonged to no one until the Darlings employed her. She lived in the nursery in her own tidy doghouse which quite suited the Darlings. (The housekeeper, Liza, was not fond of kennels in the house, but all made do.) Nana was very good with the children. No nursery could possibly have been more neat and orderly. In fact, the whole house was tip-top and the rooms were often filled with music and laughter. This simply was the happiest family—until the coming of Peter Pan.

Mrs. Darling first heard of Peter when she was tidying up her children's dreams. All good mothers do this, of course. It is quite like tidying up drawers. When you wake in the morning, the naughty and evil thoughts you went to bed with

have been folded up small and placed at the bottom of your mind—and on the top, beautifully aired, are spread out your prettier thoughts, ready for you to put on.

Of course, Mrs. Darling was surprised at first to find the name of "Peter" in her children's minds. She knew of no Peter, and yet he was here and there in John and Michael's minds, while Wendy's began to be scrawled all over with him.

"Who is he, my pet?" her mother asked.

"He is Peter Pan, you know, Mother," Wendy answered sleepily.

At first Mrs. Darling did not know what to make of this Peter. But after thinking back into her own childhood, she remembered a Peter Pan who was said to live with the fairies. There were odd stories about him, such as: when children died he went part of the way with them, so that they would not be frightened. She had believed in him at the time, but now she was a grownup and she quite doubted whether there was any such person.

There came an evening, however, when her doubts were soon enough put to rest. It happened to be Nana's evening off, and Mrs. Darling had

bathed the children and sung to them till one by one they had let go her hand and slid away into the land of sleep.

All were looking so safe and cozy that she smiled at her fears now and sat down peacefully by the fire to sew. The fire was warm and the nursery was dimly lit by three night-lights. Before long, Mrs. Darling's head nodded and she was asleep.

While she was sleeping, the window of the nursery blew open and a boy dropped on the floor. Along with him came a strange light, no bigger than your fist, which darted about the room like a living thing. I think it must have been this light that wakened Mrs. Darling.

She started up with a cry, then saw the boy. Somehow she knew at once that he was Peter Pan. He was a lovely boy, dressed in skeleton leaves and the saps that ooze out of trees. When he saw her, his lips curled into a most mischievous smile.

CHAPTER TWO

The Shadow

Mrs. Darling screamed, and Nana burst through the door. Nana growled and sprang at the boy, who leapt lightly out the window. Quickly, Mrs. Darling ran down into the street to look for his little body, but it was not there. She looked up, but in the black night she could see nothing except what she thought was a shooting star.

She returned to the nursery and found Nana with something in her mouth, which turned out to be the boy's shadow. When the boy had leapt, Nana had closed the window quickly—too late to catch *him*, but his shadow had no time to get out. Slam! went the window and snapped it off.

You may be sure Mrs. Darling examined the shadow carefully, but it was quite the ordinary kind. Mrs. Darling thought that it would be fitting to show the shadow to Mr. Darling. She rolled the shadow up and put it away carefully in a drawer, until she had a moment to tell him of the strange visitor.

The very next Friday evening, the Darlings were rushing about getting ready for a dinner

party down the street at Number 27. The children were playing noisily in their nursery and Nana was barking, trying to quiet them. Liza, who did not approve of a dog in the nursery, became quite unnerved with all the noise. As soon as the Darlings had closed the door behind them, she dragged poor Nana out into the yard and chained her up. The children lay in sad silence as they listened to Nana protest.

In the darkness they could hear Nana barking, and John whimpered, "It is because Liza chained her up in the yard."

But Wendy was wiser. "That is not Nana's *unhappy* bark," she said, "that is her bark when she smells *danger*."

"Are you sure, Wendy?" Michael asked fearfully.

"Oh, yes," Wendy replied.

Even Michael knew that Nana was bothered. He asked, "Can anything harm us, Wendy, after the night-lights are lit?"

"Nothing," she said. "They are the eyes a mother leaves behind her to guard her children."

The house at Number 27 was only a few yards distant, but there had been a slight fall of snow, so Father and Mother Darling walked carefully

so as not to soil their shoes. They were already the only persons in the street, and all the stars were watching them.

The stars were not really friendly to Peter, who often snuck up behind them and tried to blow them out. But stars love to have fun and they were on his side tonight—and anxious to get the grownups out of the way. So as soon as the door of Number 27 closed behind Mr. and Mrs. Darling, the smallest of all the stars in the Milky Way screamed out:

"Now, Peter!"

CHAPTER THREE

Of Peter and Wendy

For a moment after Mr. and Mrs. Darling left the house, the night-lights by the beds of the three children continued to burn clearly. They were awfully nice little night-lights, and it would have been nice if they could have kept awake to see Peter. But Wendy's light blinked and gave such a yawn that the other two yawned also. Before they could close their mouths, all three night-lights went out.

There was another light in the room now. This little light was a thousand times brighter than the night-lights. It moved very quickly. In no time at all, it had been in all the drawers in the

nursery. The light was looking for Peter's shadow. It shuffled through the wardrobe and turned every pocket inside out. It was not really a light. It was bright from flashing about so quickly. When it came to rest for a second you saw it was a fairy, no bigger than your hand. It was a girl called Tinker Bell. A beautiful fairy-girl who wore a gown made of a single leaf.

A moment after Tinker Bell flew into the nursery, Peter dropped in. He had carried Tinker Bell part of the way, and his hand was still messy with the fairy dust.

"Tinker Bell," he called softly. "Tink, where are you?"

She was in a jug for the moment, and liking it quite a bit. She had never been in a jug before.

"Oh, *do* come out of that jug, and tell me—do you know where they put my shadow?"

The loveliest tinkle like golden bells answered him. It is the fairy language. (You ordinary children can never hear it, but if you *were* to hear it you would know that you had heard it once before.)

Tink said that the shadow was in the big box.

She meant the chest of drawers, and Peter jumped at the drawers. He pulled them open with both hands and threw the clothes onto the floor. In a moment he had found his shadow and quickly shut the drawer. But wait! He was so excited that he shut Tinker Bell up inside!

Peter thought that he and his shadow would join again like drops of water. Surely he would only need to place the shadow near him and they would stick together like glue. But this did not work. No matter how hard he tried he could not make his shadow stick. He even tried to stick it on with soap from the bathroom, but that did no good. An ache began in Peter's stomach, and he sat on the floor and cried.

His sobs woke Wendy, and she sat up in bed. She was not surprised to see a stranger crying on the nursery floor. She was only pleasantly interested.

"Boy," she said politely, "why are you crying?"

Peter could be very polite also, having learned the grand manner at fairy ceremonies, and he rose and bowed to her beautifully. She was much pleased and bowed beautifully back to him.

"What's your name?" he asked.

"Wendy Moira Angela Darling," she replied proudly. "What is your name?"

"Peter Pan."

She was already sure that he must be Peter, but it did seem a very short name.

"Is that all?"

"Yes," he said rather sharply. He felt for the first time that perhaps it was a shortish name.

"I'm so sorry," said Wendy Moira Angela.

She asked where he lived.

"Second to the right," said Peter, "and then straight on till morning."

"What a funny address!"

Peter had a sinking feeling. For the first time he felt that perhaps it was a funny address.

"No, it isn't," he said.

"I mean," Wendy said nicely, remembering that she was hostess, "is *that* what they put on the letters?"

He wished she had not mentioned letters.

"Don't get any letters," he said scornfully.

"But doesn't your mother get letters?"

"Don't have a mother," he said.

Not only had he no mother, but he had not the slightest desire to have one. He thought they were a bother. Wendy, however, felt at once that it was a very sad and terrible thing not to have a mother.

"Oh, Peter, no wonder you were crying," she said. She got out of bed and ran to him.

"I wasn't crying about mothers," he said rather angrily. "I was crying because I can't get my shadow to stick on. Besides, I wasn't crying."

"It has come off?"

"Yes."

Then Wendy saw the shadow on the floor, looking so sad and limp, and she felt very sorry for Peter. "How awful!" she said, but she could not help smiling when she saw that he had been trying to stick it on with soap. How exactly like a boy!

Fortunately she knew at once what to do. "It must be sewn on," she said, in a rather motherish tone.

"What's sewn?" he asked.

"You are quite unschooled."

"No, I'm not."

She began at once to speak to him as if she were the grownup. "I shall sew it on for you, my little man," she said. She got out her sewing kit, and sewed the shadow onto Peter's foot.

"I dare say it will hurt a little," she warned him.

"Oh, I won't cry," said Peter, who already thought he had *never* cried in his life. He clenched his teeth and indeed did *not* cry, and soon his shadow was behaving properly, though it did have a few wrinkles.

"Perhaps I should have ironed it," Wendy said thoughtfully, but Peter did not care. He was happy to be back with his shadow and jumped about gleefully. Alas, he had already forgotten that Wendy had helped him at all. He thought he had attached the shadow himself.

"How clever I am!" he crowed happily. "Oh, the cleverness of me!"

CHAPTER FOUR

Of Kisses and Fairies

Wendy was shocked at Peter's crowing. "You are so stuck up," she sneered. "Of course, you think I did nothing!"

"You did a little," Peter said carelessly, and continued to dance.

"A little!" she scoffed. "If I am no use, I can at least withdraw," and she sprang in the most grand way into bed and covered her face with the blankets.

To try to get her to look up, Peter pretended to be going away. When this did not work, he sat on the end of the bed and tapped her gently with his foot.

"Wendy," he said, "don't be angry. I can't help crowing, Wendy, when I'm pleased with myself." Still she would not look up, though she was listening eagerly. "Wendy, one girl is more use than twenty boys."

"Do you really think so, Peter?" she asked in her most pitiful voice.

"Yes, I do."

"I think it's perfectly sweet of you," she declared, "and I'll get up again." She sat with him on the side of the bed. She also said she would give him a kiss if he liked, but Peter did not know what she meant, and he held out his hand, expecting something.

"Surely you know what a kiss is!" she asked, astonished.

"I shall know when you give it to me," he replied curtly.

Wendy did not want to hurt his feelings, so she gave him a thimble.

"Now," said he, "shall I give *you* a kiss?"

Wendy replied with a slight primness, "If you please."

She turned her face toward him, but he merely dropped an acorn button into her hand.

She slowly returned her face to where it had been before, and said nicely that she would wear his kiss on the chain around her neck. (It was lucky that she did put it on that chain, for later it would save her life.)

Wendy wondered how old Peter might be and so she asked him his age.

"I don't know," he answered uneasily, "but I am quite young. You see, I ran away the day I was born. It was because I heard father and mother talking about what I was to be when I became a man."

He was very upset now. "I don't want ever to be a man," he said. "I want always to be a little boy and to have fun. So I ran away to Kensington Gardens and lived a long, long time among the fairies."

Wendy was very impressed. Peter thought it was because he had run away, but it was really because he knew fairies. Wendy had lived at home all her life and had not been many places. She thought that it would be lovely to know a fairy. She began asking Peter loads of questions about them. Peter was surprised at this, for fairies were always getting in his way and so on. Indeed he sometimes had to give them a rap on the head!

Still, he liked them on the whole, and he told her about the beginning of fairies.

"You see, Wendy, when the first baby laughed for the first time, its laugh broke into a thousand pieces, and they all went skipping about, and that was the beginning of fairies."

Peter was bored talking of fairies, but Wendy, being a stay-at-home, liked it.

"And so," he went on sweetly, "there ought to be one fairy for every boy and girl."

"Ought to be? Isn't there?"

"No. You see, children know such a lot now, they soon don't believe in fairies. Every time a child says, 'I don't believe in fairies,' there is a fairy somewhere that falls down dead."

Really, he thought they had now talked enough about fairies, and it struck him that Tinker Bell was keeping very quiet. "I can't think where she has gone to," he said, rising, and he called Tink by name. Wendy's heart fluttered with excitement.

"Peter," she cried, "you don't mean to tell me that there is a *fairy* in this room!"

"She was here just now," he said. "You don't hear her, do you?" and they both listened.

12
11
1

"The only sound I hear," said Wendy, "is like a tinkle of bells."

"Well, that's Tink, and that's the fairy language. I think I hear her, too. She is called Tinker Bell because she is a tinker—she fixes the pots and kettles."

The sound came from the chest of drawers. Peter made a merry face and giggled like a child.

"Wendy," he whispered gleefully, "I do believe I shut her up in the drawer!"

He let poor Tink out of the drawer, and she flew about the nursery, screaming with fury.

"You shouldn't say such things," Peter scolded. "Of course I'm very sorry, but how could I know you were in the drawer?"

"Oh, Peter," Wendy cried, "if she would only stand still and let me see her!"

"They hardly ever stand still," he said, but for one moment Wendy saw the little figure come to rest on the cuckoo clock. "O the lovely!" she cried, though Tink's face was still very angry.

"Tink," said Peter kindly, "this lady says she wishes you were *her* fairy."

Tinker Bell answered rudely.

"What does she say, Peter?"

He had to translate. "She is not very polite. She says *you* are a great ugly girl, and that she is *my* fairy." Peter looked sternly at the fairy. "You have bad manners, Tink."

To this Tinker Bell replied, "You silly nincompoop," and she disappeared into the bathroom.

"She is quite a rude fairy," Peter explained.

CHAPTER FIVE

Come Away, Come Away!

They were together in the armchair now and Wendy asked him many more questions.

"If you don't live in Kensington Gardens now—"

"Sometimes I do still."

"But where do you live mostly now?"

"With the lost boys."

"Who are they?"

"They are the children who fall out of their carriages in the park when the nurse is not looking. If they are not claimed in seven days they are sent far away to the Neverland. I'm captain."

"What fun it must be!"

Wendy then asked Peter why he came to the window in the first place. He told her it was to hear the stories Mrs. Darling told. You see, none of the lost boys knew any stories.

"Oh, Wendy, your mother was telling you such a lovely story. A story about the prince who couldn't find the lady who wore the glass slipper."

"Peter," said Wendy excitedly, "that was Cinderella, and he found her, and they lived happily ever after."

Peter was so glad that he jumped up and hurried to the window.

"Where are you going?" she cried.

"To tell the other boys."

"Don't go, Peter," she pleaded, "I know such a lot of stories! Oh, the stories I could tell to the boys!"

Peter grabbed her and began to draw her toward the window. "Wendy, do come with me and tell the other boys."

Of course she was very pleased to be asked, but she said, "Oh, dear, I can't. Think of my mother! Oh, Mummy, she would miss me so! Besides, I can't fly."

"I'll teach you how to jump on the wind's back, and then away we go," said Peter.

"Oo!" she exclaimed.

"There are mermaids," Peter said.

"Mermaids! With tails?"

"Such long tails."

"Oh," cried Wendy, "I would love to see a mermaid!"

She was so excited that she danced about as if she were having trouble remaining on the nursery floor. It was quite as if she might float away on her own.

"Peter, would you teach John and Michael to fly, too?" she begged.

"If you like," he said.

She ran to John and Michael and shook them. "Wake up," she cried. "Peter Pan has come and he is to teach us to fly."

John rubbed his eyes. "Then I shall get up," he said. "Hallo. What's this about flying?"

Michael woke up too and asked what the excitement was about. Peter suddenly whispered for them to be quiet. All was as still as salt. Nana, who had been barking all evening, was quiet now. Something was up.

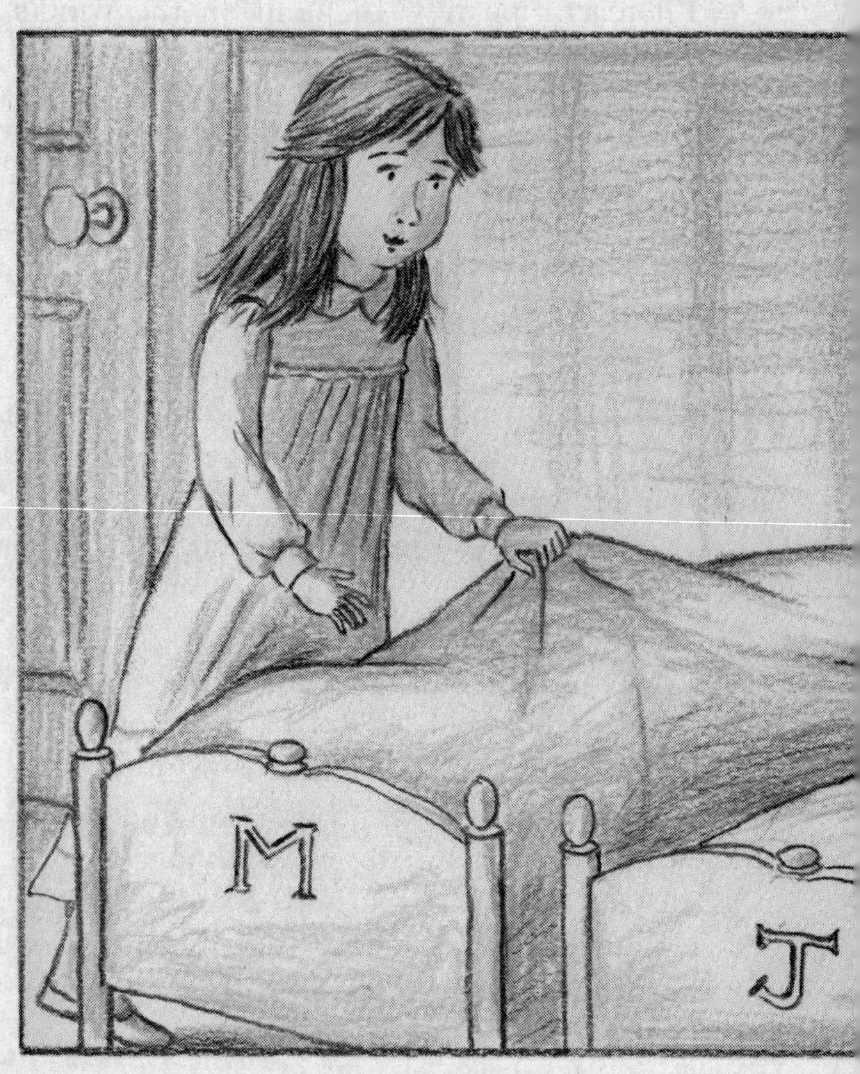
M
J

"Out with the light! Hide! Quick!" cried John.

And so, when Liza entered, holding Nana, the nursery seemed quite its old self, very dark, and very quiet.

Liza was in a bad temper. "There, you silly dog," she said, "they are perfectly safe, aren't they? Every one of the little angels is sound asleep in bed. Listen to their gentle breathing."

Indeed, the three angels were really standing behind the window curtains! Michael breathed so loudly that they were nearly found out. Nana knew that kind of breathing, and she tried to drag herself out of Liza's arms.

"No more of it, Nana," Liza said sternly, pulling her out of the room. "I warn you, if you bark again I shall go straight for master and missus and bring them home from the party, and then, oh, won't master punish you!"

She tied the unhappy dog up again outside, but do you think Nana stopped barking? Bring master and missus home from the party! Why, that was just what Nana wanted. Do you think she cared whether she was punished so long as the children were safe? She barked even louder!

But Liza paid no attention. Nana, seeing that no help would come, strained at the chain until at last she broke it.

In another moment, Nana had burst into the dining room of Number 27 and flung up her paws. Mr. and Mrs. Darling knew at once that something terrible was happening in their nursery. Without a good-bye to their hostess, they rushed into the street.

But it was now ten minutes since three naughty children had been breathing behind the curtains, and Peter Pan can do a great deal in ten minutes.

We now return to the nursery.

"It's all right," John announced, coming out from his hiding place. "I say, Peter, can you really fly?"

Instead of troubling to answer him, Peter flew around the room, performing cartwheels in mid-air.

"How topping!" said John and Michael.

"How sweet!" cried Wendy.

"Yes, I'm sweet, oh, I am sweet!" said Peter, forgetting his manners again.

It looked delightfully easy, and they tried it first from the floor and then from the beds, but they always went down instead of up.

"I say, how do you do it?" asked John, rubbing his knee.

"Fairy dust, of course," Peter said, "for no one can fly unless the fairy dust has been blown on him."

As we told you earlier, one of his hands was messy with fairy dust, and he blew some on each of them. The results were most superb.

"Now just wiggle your shoulders this way," he said, "and let go."

They were all on their beds. They dared Michael to let go first and all at once he had flown across the room.

"I flewed!" he screamed while still in mid-air.

John let go and met Wendy near the bathroom.

"Oh, lovely!"

"Oh, ripping!"

"Look at me!"

"Look at me!"

"Look at me!"

They were not nearly so elegant as Peter. They could not help kicking a little, and their heads were knocking against the ceiling. Up and down they went, and round and round.

"I say," cried John, "why shouldn't we all go out?"

Michael was ready. He wanted to see how long it took him to do a billion miles. But Wendy hesitated.

"Mermaids!" said Peter again.

"Oo!"

"And there are pirates."

"Pirates!" cried John, grabbing his Sunday hat. "Let us go at once."

It was just at this moment that Mr. and Mrs. Darling and Nana arrived outside the door of Number 14. From the street they could see four shadows flying around the nursery. Quick as lightning, they opened the door and rushed upstairs. But it was too late. When the Darlings and Nana arrived at the nursery door, the window was open and the children and Peter had flown away into the night.

CHAPTER SIX

The Flight

"Second to the right, and straight on till morning."

That, Peter had told Wendy, was the way to the Neverland—but even birds could not have found it with these instructions. Peter, you see, just said anything that came into his head.

At first they all had a smashing good time, flying in great circles in the air. John and Michael raced, Michael getting a head start. They told one another that they were superb flyers, even though they had only learned to fly a short while ago.

Sometimes it was dark and sometimes light, and now they were very cold and then too warm. Did they really feel hungry at times, or were they

merely pretending? It seemed that they had been flying for days, but maybe it had only been a few hours.

Indeed the three children were not sure of the time, nor did they seem to care. They had a wonderful time playing follow-the-leader, swooping down to touch shark fins in the ocean or zooming up to play tag with the stars. Finally, Peter cried in his captain voice, “We get off here.”

Below them was Neverland!

“Where, where?” the children cried at once.

“Where all the arrows are pointing.”

Indeed a million golden arrows were pointing it out to the children, all directed by their friend the sun, who wanted them to be sure of their way before leaving them for the night.

Wendy and John and Michael stood on tiptoe in the air to get their first sight of the island. Strange to say, they all recognized it at once.

“John, there’s the lagoon,” said Wendy.

“Wendy, look at the turtles burying their eggs in the sand.”

“I say, John, I see the smoke of the Injun camp!”

“Where? Show me, and I’ll tell you by the way the smoke curls if they are on the warpath.”

"There, just across the Mysterious River."

"I see now. Yes, they are on the warpath right enough," said John.

The island seemed scary to them in the coming darkness. They had been flying apart, but they huddled close to Peter now. His eyes

were sparkling, and a tingle went through the children every time they touched his body. They were now over the fearsome island, flying so low that sometimes a tree touched their feet.

Peter put his hand to his ear and listened carefully. He was not afraid of anything.

"Would you like an adventure now," he said to John, "or would you like to have your tea first?"

"What kind of adventure?" John asked carefully.

"There's a pirate asleep in the forest just beneath us," Peter told him. "If you like, we'll go down and 'get' him."

"Suppose," John said, a little timidly, "he were to wake up?"

Peter spoke angrily. "You don't think I would hurt him while he was sleeping! I would wake him first, and then get him. That's the way I always do."

John said, "How ripping," but decided to have tea first. He asked if there were many pirates on the island just now, and Peter said there had never been so many.

"Who is captain now?"

"Hook," answered Peter, and his face became very stern as he said that hated word.

"James Hook?"

"Aye."

Then indeed Michael began to cry, and even John could speak in gulps only, for they knew that Hook was evil.

"He was Blackbeard's boatswain," John whispered. "He is the worst of them all."

"That's him," said Peter.

"What's he like? Is he big?"

"He is not as big as he was."

"How do you mean?"

"I cut off a bit of him," Peter bragged.

"But, I say, what bit?" John asked.

"His right hand."

"Then he can't fight now?"

"Oh, can't he just! He has an iron hook instead of a right hand, and he claws with it."

"Claws!" Michael cried.

"I say, John," said Peter.

"Yes."

"Say, 'Aye, aye, sir.' "

"Aye, aye, sir."

"There is one thing," Peter continued, "that every boy who serves under me has to promise, and so must you."

John grew pale.

"It is this: If we meet Hook in open fight, you must leave him to me."

"I promise," John said with relief.

Tinker Bell was flying about in quick circles, which lit their faces nicely.

"Tink tells me," said Peter, "that the pirates sighted us before the darkness came, and got Long Tom out."

"The big gun?"

"Yes, and of course they must see Tink's light. If they guess we are near it, they are sure to fire the cannon at us."

"Tell her to go away at once, Peter," the three cried at once.

But he would not. "She thinks we have lost the way," he replied, "and she is frightened. You don't think I would send her away all by herself when she is frightened!"

For a moment the circle of light was broken, and something gave Peter a loving little pinch.

"Then tell her," Wendy begged, "to put out her light."

"She can't put it out. That is about the only thing fairies can't do. It just goes out by itself

when she falls asleep, same as the stars."

"Then tell her to sleep at once," John almost ordered.

"She can't sleep except when she's sleepy. It is the only *other* thing fairies can't do."

"Seems to me," growled John, "these are the only two things worth doing."

Here *he* got a pinch, but not a loving one.

"If only one of us had a pocket," Peter said, "we could carry her in it." However, they had set off in such a hurry that there was not a pocket between the four of them.

Peter had a happy idea. John's hat!

Tink agreed to travel by hat if it was carried in the hand. Wendy took the hat, and this, as we shall see, led to mischief, for Tinker Bell had hoped to be carried by Peter—and she was already quite jealous of Wendy.

In the black top hat her light was completely hidden, and they flew on in silence. It was the stillest silence they had ever known.

"If only something would make a sound!" Michael cried.

As if in answer to his request, the most tremendous crash he had ever heard filled the air.

The pirates had fired Long Tom at them! The roar of this great cannon echoed through the mountains.

All of the children were scattered in the air by the blast. When everything was quiet again they called to one another.

"Are you shot?" John whispered in a shaky voice.

"I haven't checked yet," Michael whispered back.

We know now that no one had been hit. Peter, however, had been carried by the wind of the shot far out to sea, while Wendy was blown upward with Tinker Bell.

It would have been better for Wendy if at that moment she had dropped the hat.

You see, Tink hated Wendy with all her heart. She was jealous because Peter liked Wendy so much and brought the silly girl to Neverland to join the adventures. The naughty fairy began to lead Wendy away from the others into the darkness. She began to speak to Wendy and dart about her head. What she said in her lovely tinkle Wendy could not understand. I believe some of it was bad words, but it sounded kind. She flew

back and forward, plainly meaning "Follow me, and all will be well."

What else could poor Wendy do? She called to Peter and John and Michael, and got only her echoes in reply. She did not yet know that Tink hated her with a fierce hatred. And so, scared and confused, she followed Tink to her doom.

CHAPTER SEVEN

The Island Come True

Feeling that Peter was on his way back, the Neverland had again woke into life. The lost boys were out looking for Peter, the pirates were out looking for the lost boys, the Indians were out looking for the pirates, and the beasts were out looking for the Indians. They were going round and round the island, but they did not meet because all were going at the same rate.

The boys were not thinking of the pirates, the Indians or the beasts. They were out to greet their captain. There are six of them—counting the twins as two. Each is dressed in a bear skin and is full of high spirits.

Here they come now! Let us name each one!

The first is Tootles, not the least brave but the most unlucky of the band. (Poor Tootles, there is danger in the air for you tonight. Beware of Tinker Bell!) Next comes Nibs, the joyful and carefree. He is followed by Slightly, who cuts whistles out of the trees and dances with delight to his own tunes. Curly is fourth. He is a pickle, and so often in trouble. Last come the Twins, who cannot be described because we might be describing the wrong one. Peter could never tell the Twins apart, and so to avoid trouble for themselves (as Peter is quite unpleasant when he does not know something), they answer as one.

The boys disappear in the gloom. But in a short while we hear voices. It must be the pirates looking for the lost boys. We hear them before they are seen, and it is always the same dreadful song:

Avast, belay, yo ho, heave to,
A-pirating we go,
And if we're parted by a shot
We're sure to meet below!

A more mean-looking gang never existed. Here is Cecco with his great strong arms. Now comes Bill Jukes who wears one hundred tattoos. Cookson, Gentleman Starkey, and Skylights come next, singing and growling into the darkness. The Irish boatswain Smee and the laughing Alf Mason are sharing a pipe and looking behind every tree for the lost boys. Let us not forget Noodler, whose hands were fixed on backwards and who is as mean as any of the band.

In the middle of them, the blackest and largest of the group, is James Hook.

He was seated in a chariot drawn by his men. Instead of a right hand he had the iron hook. In person he was ghostly white, and an evil air hung about him like a mist. His hair was dressed in long thick curls, which at a distance looked like black snakes that wriggled around his handsome face. His eyes were a dancing blue and had a certain sadness—except when he was plunging his hook into you; *and then*, two red spots appeared in his eyes that lit them up horribly!

Something of the grand charm still clung to him, so that he even *fought* with a fanciful air. A man of great courage, it was said that the only thing he drew back from was the sight of his own blood, which was thick and of an unusual color. In fashion he always chose the clothing of a duke or lord—with great neckerchiefs of snow white lace and velvet overcoats. In his mouth he had a holder of his own invention which enabled him to smoke two cigars at once. But the grimmest and most terrifying part of him was his iron claw.

On the trail of the pirates, on their silent warpath, come the Indians. They carry tomahawks and knives, and their bodies gleam with paint and oil, for these Indians are the Piccaninny tribe. In the midst of them is the brave Great Big Little Panther. Bringing up the rear, the place of greatest danger, comes Princess Tiger Lily, proudly walking tall. She is the most beautiful of all the Indian princesses, and a mighty warrior who could equal any brave. Observe how they pass over fallen twigs without making the slightest noise.

The Indians disappear like shadows, and soon their place is taken by the beasts. Lions, tigers and bears, and the many smaller savage things that flee from them. When they have passed, there comes the last figure of all—a gigantic crocodile!

We shall see just what it seeks very soon.

The crocodile passes, but soon the boys appear again and they fling themselves down on the grassy hill, close to their underground home.

"I do wish Peter would come back," every one of them said nervously.

To pass the time and stay their fright, they talked of Cinderella, and Tootles was confident that his mother must have been very much like her. It was only when Peter was away that they could speak of mothers. Peter said that talk of mothers was silly—and would not allow it.

* * * * * * CHAPTER EIGHT * * * * * *

Of Pirates and Wendy Birds

While they talked they heard a distant sound. It was the grim song:

Yo ho, yo ho, the pirate life,
The flag o' skull and bones,
A merry hour, a hempen rope,
And hey for Davy Jones.

At once the lost boys—but where are they? They are no longer there. Rabbits could not have disappeared more quickly. I will tell you where they are. Nibs has sped off to spy, but the others are already in their home under the ground. But how have they reached it? For there is no entrance to be seen. Look closely, however, and you may note seven large trees, each with a hole in its hollow trunk as large as a boy. These are the entrances to the home under the ground. They are very well hidden, and Hook has never found them.

As the pirates moved closer, the quick eye of Starkey sighted Nibs disappearing through the woods, and at once his pistol flashed out. But an iron claw gripped his shoulder.

"Captain, let go!" he cried.

Now for the first time we hear the voice of Hook. It was a black and murky voice. "Put back that pistol first," it said.

"It was one of those boys you hate. I could have wounded him," said Starkey.

"Aye, and the sound would have brought Tiger Lily's Injuns upon us."

"Shall I go after the boy, Captain," asked Smee, "and tickle him with Johnny Corkscrew?" His blade was named Johnny Corkscrew because he wiggled it in the wound.

"Not now, Smee," Hook said darkly. "He is only one, and I want to mischief all the boys. Scatter and look for them."

The pirates disappeared among the trees, and in a moment their Captain and the boatswain Smee were alone.

"Most of all," Hook was saying, "I want their captain, Peter Pan. It was he who cut off my hand." He waved the hook. "I've waited long to shake his hand with this. Oh, I'll tear him! Peter flung my arm," he said with a wince, "to a crocodile that happened to be passing by."

"I have often noticed your strange dread of crocodiles," said Smee.

"Not of crocodiles," Hook corrected him, "but of that *one* crocodile." He lowered his voice. "It liked my arm so much, Smee, that it has followed me ever since, licking its lips for the rest of me." Hook growled. "I want Peter Pan, who first gave that crock its taste for me."

He sat down on a large mushroom, and now there was a quiver in his voice. "Smee," he said, "that crocodile would have had me before this, but, by a lucky chance, it swallowed a clock which goes *tick tick tick tick* inside it. And so, before it can reach me I hear the tick and run."

He laughed, but in a sad sort of way.

Then Hook realized he was feeling warm. “Smee,” he said, “this seat is hot.” He jumped up. “Odds bobs, hammer and tongs! I’m burning!”

They looked at the mushroom and then they tried to pull it up. It came away at once in their hands, for it had no root. Strangely, smoke began to rise out from the ground. The pirates looked at each other.

“A chimney!” they both exclaimed.

They had indeed discovered the chimney of the home under the ground. The boys always stopped it up with a mushroom when enemies were in the neighborhood.

Not only smoke came out of it. There came also children's voices, for the boys felt so safe in their hiding place that they were happily chattering. The pirates listened grimly, and then replaced the mushroom. They looked around and noted the holes in the seven trees.

"Did you hear them say Peter Pan's away from home?" Smee whispered.

Hook nodded. A curdling smile lit up his dark face.

"Let us return to the ship," Hook replied slowly through his teeth, "and then we will..." He stopped suddenly and cocked an ear to the wind. Faintly, ever so faintly, the sound of ticking could be heard beneath the gentle breeze.

Tick tick tick tick!

Hook stood shuddering, his breath frozen in his chest. "The crocodile!" he gasped, and bounded away, followed by his boatswain.

It was indeed the crocodile. It slithered on after Hook.

Once more the boys emerged into the open and began their nightly games of hide-and-seek. It was Nibs who first saw a strange white object fluttering in the sky and came out from his hiding place to tell the others.

"I have seen a wonderfuller thing," he cried, as they gathered round him eagerly. "A great white bird. It is flying this way."

"What kind of a bird, do you think?"

"I don't know," Nibs said, in awe, "but it looks so weary, and as it flies it moans, 'Poor Wendy.' "

"Poor Wendy?"

"I remember," said Slightly, who was always pretending to know everything, "there are birds called Wendies."

"See, it comes!" cried Curly, pointing to Wendy in the sky.

Wendy was now almost overhead, and they could hear her sorrowful cry. But they could also hear the shrill voice of Tinker Bell. The jealous fairy no longer acted like Wendy's friend. She was darting at Wendy from every direction, pinching her. (She truly did hate her!)

"Hullo, Tink," called the boys.

Tink's reply rang out:

"Peter wants you to shoot the Wendy."

They did not question an order from Peter. "Let us do what Peter wishes!" cried the brainless boys. "Quick, bows and arrows!"

All but Tootles popped down their trees. He already had a bow and arrow with him, and Tink saw it, and rubbed her little hands.

"Quick, Tootles, quick!" she screamed. "Peter will be so pleased."

Tootles excitedly fitted the arrow to his bow. "Out of the way, Tink," he shouted, and then he fired, and Wendy fluttered to the ground with an arrow in her chest.

CHAPTER NINE

Peter Returns

Foolish Tootles was standing like a hero over Wendy's body when the other boys sprang from their trees.

"You are too late," he cried proudly. "I have shot the Wendy Bird. Peter will be so pleased with me."

Overhead, Tinker Bell shouted, "Silly nincompoop!" and darted into hiding. The others did not hear her. They had crowded around Wendy. As they looked, a terrible silence fell upon them.

Slightly was the first to speak. "This is no bird," he said in a scared voice. "I think this must be a lady."

"A lady?" said Tootles, and fell a-trembling.

"And we have killed her," Nibs said hoarsely.

They all snatched off their caps.

"Now I see," Curly said. "Peter was bringing her to us." He threw himself sorrowfully on the ground.

"A lady to take care of us at last," said one of the Twins, "and you have killed her!"

They were sorry for him, but sorrier for themselves. They all stepped away from Tootles.

Tootles' face was very white. "I did it," he said. He moved slowly away.

"Don't go," they called, feeling sorry for him.

"I must," he answered, shaking. "I am so afraid of Peter."

It was at this sad moment that they heard a sound that made their hearts freeze with fright. They heard Peter crow.

"Peter!" they cried. (For he always crowed to signal his return.)

"Hide her," they whispered.

They quickly gathered around Wendy.

Tootles stood alone.

Again came that ringing crow, and Peter dropped in front of them. The boys were silent.

"Greetings, boys," he cried.

Then again was silence.

He frowned.

"I am back," he said hotly. "Why do you not cheer?"

They opened their mouths, but the cheers would not come. Peter went on talking anyway.

"Great news, boys," he cried. "I have brought at last a mother for you all."

Still no sound, except a little thud from Tootles as he dropped on his knees.

"Have you not seen her?" asked Peter, becoming troubled. "She flew this way."

"Ah me!" one voice said, and another said, "Oh, sad day."

Tootles got up. "Peter," he said quietly, "I will show her to you. Step back, Twins. Let Peter see."

So they all stood back, and let him see, and after he had looked for a little time he did not know what to do next.

"Whose arrow?" he demanded sternly.

"Mine, Peter," said Tootles on his knees.

"Oh, cruel hand," Peter said, as he stepped toward Tootles.

"Wait!" cried Nibs. "See her arm! It moves!"

Wonderful to say, Wendy had raised her arm. Nibs bent over her. "I think she said, 'Poor Tootles,' " he whispered.

"She lives," Peter said.

Slightly cried joyfully, "The Wendy lady lives."

Then Peter knelt beside her and found his acorn button. You remember she had put it on a chain that she wore round her neck.

"See," he said, "the arrow struck against this. It is the kiss I gave her. It has saved her life."

"I remember kisses," Slightly said quickly, as if he knew. "Let me see it. Aye, that's a kiss."

Peter did not hear him. He was begging Wendy to get better quickly, so that he could show her the mermaids. Of course she could not answer yet (being still in a frightful faint), but from overhead came a sobbing sound.

"Listen to Tink," said Curly. "She is crying because the Wendy lives."

Then they had to tell Peter of Tink's crime, and almost never had they seen him look so angry.

"Listen, Tinker Bell," he cried, "I am your friend no more. Be gone from me forever."

She flew onto his shoulder and pleaded, but he brushed her off. Not until Wendy again raised her arm did he soften enough to say, "Well, not forever, but for a whole week."

Do you think Tinker Bell was grateful to Wendy for raising her arm? Oh, dear, *no*! The mean little fairy never wanted to pinch her so much. Fairies indeed are strange.

"Let us carry Wendy down into the house," Curly suggested.

"No," cried Peter. "We must fetch a doctor."

In a moment they were all scurrying around like ants, looking for a doctor. But where were they to find a doctor on the island? While they were at it, who should appear but John and Michael. As the two boys dragged along the ground, they fell asleep standing—stopped—woke up—moved another step—and slept again.

"John, John," Michael would cry, "wake up! Where is Nana, John? And Mother?"

And then John would rub his eyes and mutter, "It is true, we did fly."

They were very relieved to find Peter.

"Hullo, Peter," they said.

"Hullo," replied Peter, though he had quite forgotten them. He was very busy at the moment taking care of Wendy.

"Is Wendy asleep?" John and Michael asked.

"Yes."

"John," Michael said, "let us wake her and get her to make supper for us." But as he said it, some of the other boys rushed in carrying water and leaves to make bandages. "Look at them!" Michael cried.

"Curly," said Peter in his most captainy voice, "see that these boys help in the search for a doctor."

"Aye, aye, sir."

"A doctor!" exclaimed John.

"For the Wendy," said Curly.

"For Wendy?" John cried. "Why, you said she was asleep. Just wake her up!"

Peter frowned. "Slightly," he cried, "you must be a doctor."

"Aye, aye," said Slightly at once, and disappeared, scratching his head, for he knew Peter must be obeyed. He returned in a moment, wearing John's hat and looking serious.

"Please, sir," said Peter, going to him, "are you a doctor?"

"Yes, my little man," Slightly pretended.

"Please, sir," Peter explained, "a lady lies very ill."

"I will put a glass thing in her mouth," said Slightly, and he made-believe to do it, while Peter waited.

"How is she?" inquired Peter.

"Tut, tut, tut," said Slightly, "this has cured her."

"I am glad!" Peter cried.

"I will call again in the evening," Slightly said. "Give her beef tea out of a cup."

"Peter!" shouted one of the boys. "She is moving in her sleep."

"Her mouth opens," cried a third. "Oh, lovely!"

"Perhaps she is going to sing in her sleep," said Peter.

She looked quite surprised, and this was just how they had hoped she would look.

"Where am I?" she said.

"You are in Neverland," Peter told her, "and these are the lost boys."

"You can be our mother!" Tootles shouted.

"And we can be your children," cried the Twins.

Then all went on their knees, and holding out their arms cried, "O Wendy lady, be our mother."

"Should I?" Wendy said, all shining. "But you see I am only a little girl."

"That doesn't matter," said Peter, as if he were the only person who knew all about it, though he was really the one who knew the least. "What we need is just a nice motherly person."

"Oh, dear!" Wendy said. "You see, I feel that is exactly what I am."

"It is, it is," they all cried. "We saw it at once."

"Very well," she said, "I will do my best. Let us go home at once, you naughty children. I am sure your feet are damp. And before I put you to bed I have just time to finish the story of Cinderella."

So into their trees they went and down into their underground home. And that was the first of the many joyous evenings they had with Wendy. The house under the ground was so cozy and safe in the darkness, with such bright singing and laughter, and Peter standing on guard in the night.

* * * * * * CHAPTER TEN * * * * * *

The Happy Home Under the Ground

One of the first things Peter did next day was to measure Wendy and John and Michael for their very own hollow trees. It was very important to have a tree of your own. Unless your tree fit you it was difficult to go up and down, and no two of the boys were quite the same size. Once you fit your tree, you sucked in your breath at the top of the tree—and down you went at exactly the right speed. To go *up* you breathed in and then out, again and again, and so wriggled up like a worm. Of course, when you have practiced enough you are able to do this quite easily—and nothing can be more graceful.

But you simply *must* fit, and Peter measures you for your tree just as you would be measured for a suit of clothes. The difference, however, is that clothes are made to fit *you*, while *you* have to be made to fit a tree. Sometimes you will have to wear a few more clothes—or a few less. And if you are bumpy in places or the only available tree is an odd shape, Peter does some things to you, and after that you fit. After a few days of practice, John, Wendy, and Michael could go up and down as easily as buckets in a well.

All three grew to love their home under the ground—especially Wendy. It had one large room with a floor in which you could dig for worms if you wanted to go fishing. In this floor grew stout mushrooms, which were used as stools. A Never tree tried hard to grow in the center of the room, and by tea time it was always about two feet high. The boys then put a door on top of it, and it became a table. As soon as they cleared the dishes away, they sawed off the trunk and thus there was more room to play.

There was one cubby-hole in the wall, no larger than a birdcage, which was the private

apartment of Tinker Bell. It had a tiny curtain which Tink, who was most private, always kept drawn when dressing or undressing. Her apartment was quite pretty and had lovely pieces of small furniture—although it did have a rather snobbish look to it.

Wendy loved the household duties such as keeping the socks mended and the kettle on for tea. The cooking also pleased her, but with Peter one never knew if the meal would be real or make-believe, and this sometimes became a bother.

Wendy's favorite time for sewing and mending was after the boys had all gone to bed. Then, she had a breathing time for herself. She made new things for them and put patches on the knees of their britches, for they were all most frightfully hard on their knees.

As time went on, did she spend any time thinking about the beloved parents she had left behind her? This is hard to say, for Time in Neverland is not the same as Time in London. But I am afraid that Wendy did not really worry about her father and mother. She was sure they would *always* keep the window open for when she would fly back—and this gave her peace of mind.

The boys had adventures of some sort every day. Peter could always lead them into a fine adventure or invent wonderful games that could be used in the place of a true adventure.

There were many times when Peter would leave the boys behind and go out alone. When he came back, they were never certain whether he had had an adventure or not. Sometimes he came home with his head bandaged, and then Wendy fussed over him and nursed his wound, while he

told a dazzling tale. But she was never quite sure, you know. There were, however, many adventures which she knew to be true because she was in them herself, and there were still more that were at least partly true, for the other boys were in them and said they were all true.

Of course, besides the adventures there were many wonders on the island such as the mermaids and the lagoon. Oh, my! the lagoon is a wonderful and magical place. If you shut your eyes and are a lucky one, you may be able to picture this place—a shapeless pool of lovely pale colors floating in the darkness. Then if you squeeze your eyes even tighter, the pool begins to take shape, and the colors become so bright that with another squeeze they burst into flames. But just before they do, you see the lagoon. Can you see the surf? Can you hear the mermaids singing?

On the island, the most lovely time to see the mermaids is at the turn of the moon, when they sing their strange and mystical songs. But the lagoon is dangerous for humans at night. (Wendy had never seen the lagoon by moonlight, not because she was afraid but because she had a strict rule of bedtime by seven o'clock.) She was often at the lagoon, however, on sunny days after rain, when the mermaids come up to play with their bubbles and the rainbow. They use these pretty bubbles as balls. Each mermaid hits a ball happily to another with her tail and tries to keep it in the rainbow till it bursts. There is a goal at each end of the rainbow, and the goal tenders are the only ones allowed to use their hands. Sometimes a dozen of these games will be going on in the lagoon at one time. It is quite a pretty sight.

CHAPTER ELEVEN

Marooner's Rock

In the middle of the lagoon rests a small rocky island called Marooner's Rock. There were stories of how evil pirates and captains had left sailors on this great rock with no boat to get back to shore! Here the marooned sailors watched as the tide rose around them—an awful thought, indeed. Yet, it was here one day that all the children were sunning themselves, lazily dozing, and Wendy was very busy, stitching.

While she stitched, a change came to the lagoon. Little shivers ran over it, and the sun went away and shadows stole across the water, turning it cold. Wendy could no longer see to thread her needle, and when she looked up, the happy lagoon seemed dreadful and unfriendly.

She knew that night had not come, but something as *dark* as night had come—or at least it was coming, and this sent shivers through the sea. What was it?

There was one on the rock who could sniff danger even in his sleep. Peter sprang straight up, as wide-awake at once as a dog. With one warning cry he woke the others.

He stood very still, one hand to his ear.

"Pirates!" he cried. The others came closer to him. A strange smile was on his face. Wendy saw it and shuddered. Peter's order came sharply.

"Dive!"

All the children slipped into the water and Marooner's Rock stood alone in the lagoon.

A boat drew near. It was a small boat, with three people aboard—Smee and Starkey, and Tiger Lily, the Indian princess! They had caught her sneaking aboard the pirate ship with a knife in her mouth. Her hands and ankles were tied, and she knew what was to be her fate. She was to be left on the rock to drown. Yet her face was proud and brave.

The two pirates did not see the rock till they crashed into it.

"Drat, you lubber!" cried Smee. "Here's the rock. Now, then, what we have to do is to leave the Injun here to drown."

The beautiful Tiger Lily did not try to escape and the pirates easily plopped her onto the rock.

Quite near the rock, but out of sight, two heads were bobbing up and down—Peter's and Wendy's. Peter was angry that it was two against one and he decided to save the princess. Peter could do almost anything—so he made himself sound like Captain Hook.

"Ahoy there, you lubbers!" he called. It was a very good Hook voice.

"The captain!" said the pirates, staring at each other in surprise.

"He must be swimming out to us," Starkey said, peering into the darkness.

"We are putting the Injun on the rock," Smee called out.

"Set her free," came the answer.

"Free?"

"Yes. Cut her ropes and let her go."

"But, Captain—"

"At once, do you hear," cried Peter, "or I'll plunge my hook in you."

"Better do what the captain orders," said Starkey nervously.

"Aye, aye," Smee said, and he cut Tiger Lily's ropes. At once like an eel she slid between Starkey's legs and into the water.

Suddenly another voice rang out over the lagoon. "Boat ahoy!" It was Hook's voice, and this time it was not Peter who had spoken.

Peter's face puckered in a whistle of surprise.

"Boat ahoy!" came the voice again.

Now Wendy understood. The real Hook was also in the water. He was swimming to the little boat. His men showed a light to guide him and he soon reached them. In the light of the lantern, Wendy saw his hook grip the boat's side and she saw his evil dark face as he pulled himself from the water. She was shaking and would have liked to swim away, but Peter would not budge. He was tingling with adventure!

The captain sat in the boat with his head on his hook, looking quite sad.

"The game's up," he cried. "Those boys have found a mother."

"O rotten luck!" cried Starkey.

"Captain," said Smee, "could we not kidnap these boys' mother and make her *our* mother?"

"That may be an idea," cried Hook. "We will seize the children and carry them to the boat. We will make the boys walk the plank, and Wendy shall be our mother."

Wendy forgot herself. "Never!" she cried.

"What was that?"

But they could see nothing. They thought it must have been a leaf in the wind. "Do you agree, my bullies?" asked Hook.

They all agreed. By this time they were on the rock, and suddenly Hook remembered Tiger Lily.

"Where is the Injun?" he demanded.

Smee and Starkey, of course, thought he was being funny.

"That is all right, Captain," Smee answered casually. "We let her go."

"Let her go?" cried Hook.

" 'Twas your own orders," Smee said.

"You called over the water to us to let her go," said Starkey.

"Brimstone and gall!" thundered Hook. "What is going on here?" His face had gone black with rage. "I gave no such order."

They were all very uncomfortable, to say the least.

Peter could no longer contain his pride and he crowed with joy, "It was I, the most clever of boys! Peter Pan!"

"Pan! Now we have him!" Hook shouted. "Into the water, Smee. Starkey, mind the boat. Take him dead or alive!"

* * * * * * CHAPTER TWELVE * * * * * *

The Battle on the Lagoon

Hook leapt into the water for the fight. Out rang Peter's mischievous voice. "Are you ready, boys?"

"Aye, aye," came replies from around the lagoon.

"Then lay into the pirates."

The fight was short and sharp. John bravely climbed into the boat and held Starkey. There was a fierce struggle. Starkey lost his cutlass and he wriggled overboard, but John leapt after him.

Here and there were flashes of steel and whoops and hollers as the boys and the pirates clashed. Smee's "corkscrew" injured Tootles, but

Curly got him right back. Farther from the rock, Starkey was battling Slightly and the Twins hard.

Where all this time was Peter? He was seeking Hook! Peter was the only one who did not fear the claw.

Where should these two meet but on Marooner's Rock! They each came up a side, and met at the top—face to face. Peter snatched a knife from Hook's belt. He was about to ask Hook to give up when he saw that he was higher up the rock than his enemy. This he knew was not fair fighting. He gave the pirate a hand to help him up.

It was then that Hook bit him.

Peter stared at Hook, horrified! It was not the pain that upset him. It was the unfair act! Hook saw his chance and struck quickly. Twice the iron hand clawed him. But then, to Peter's surprise, Hook leapt into the water.

The other boys saw Hook in the water swimming wildly for the big pirate ship—white with fear. Right behind him was the crocodile. Right behind the croc were Smee and Starkey.

The boys cheered and then began to search for each other. They found the small boat and squeezed in. But they had lost Peter and Wendy. They paddled for shore shouting "Peter! Wendy!" as they went, but no answer came.

"They must be swimming back or flying," the boys decided. They were not very worried, because they had such faith in Peter. Little did they know that Peter and Wendy were stranded in the middle of the lagoon on Marooner's Rock!

And how did Peter and Wendy get off the dreaded Marooner's Rock? Ah, well, that is indeed another tale, but I'll give you some wonderful hints. Wendy grabbed hold of Michael's kite as it drifted over the lagoon and she floated her way to shore. Peter made use of a large bird's nest (I told you these were only hints and not the full tale!) and paddled himself to safety.

All quite simple, really.

Of course the boys celebrated when Peter reached the home under the ground. Wendy showed up just after that, for she had been carried hither and thither by the kite. Every boy had adventures to tell, but perhaps the biggest adventure of all was that they were several hours late for bed. Wendy, though joyful in having them all home again safe and sound, was horrified at

how late it was. "To bed, to bed," she announced in a voice that had to be obeyed. All was back to normal in the home under the ground.

The Indians were greatly pleased about the rescue of Princess Tiger Lily. It was indeed a thrilling act of bravery. Peter and Tiger Lily became fast friends after their adventure, and now there was nothing she and her braves would not do for him. All night the tribe sat above, keeping watch over the home under the ground and awaiting the next big attack by the pirates.

CHAPTER THIRTEEN

Wendy's Story

We have now come to the part of our story that will always be called the Night of Nights. Nothing much had happened that day. That evening, the Indians in their blankets were camped up above. Below, the children were having their evening meal—all except Peter, who had gone out to get the time. (The way you got the time on the island was to find the crocodile, and then stay near him till the clock struck the hour.)

While Wendy sewed, the boys played around her. Oh, such a group of happy faces and happy dancing. The home under the ground was often a place of fun, but we are looking on it for the last time.

There were footsteps above, and Wendy was the first to hear it.

"Children, I hear Peter's step. He likes you to meet him at the door."

The excited boys dragged him from his tree. He had brought nuts for the boys as well as the correct time for Wendy.

"Peter, you just spoil them, you know," Wendy said. The boys all gathered round to feast on the delicious nuts before dressing for bed.

None of them knew what lay ahead that night. Perhaps it was best not to know. They sang and danced in their nightgowns and then at last they all got into bed for Wendy's story.

It was the story they loved best—the story Peter hated. (Usually when she began to tell this story he left the room or put his hands over his ears. But tonight he remained on his stool.)

Wendy settled down to her story, with little Michael and the other seven boys all 'round.

"There was once a gentleman…"

"I had rather he had been a lady," Curly said.

"I wish he had been a white rat," said Nibs.

"Quiet," their mother warned them. "There was a lady also, and…"

"Oh, Mummy," cried the first Twin, "you mean that there *is* a lady also, don't you? She is not dead, is she?"

"Oh, no!"

"Little less noise there," Peter called out.

"The gentleman's name," Wendy continued, "was Mr. Darling, and her name was Mrs. Darling."

"I knew them," John said, to annoy the others.

"I think I knew them," said Michael.

"They were married, you know," explained Wendy, "and what do you think they had?"

"White rats!" cried Nibs.

"No."

"They had three children!" said Tootles, who knew the story by heart.

Wendy continued, "Now these three children had a faithful nurse called Nana, but Liza, the housekeeper, was angry with her and chained her up in the yard, and so the three flew away to the Neverland, where the lost children are."

"Oh, Wendy," cried Tootles, "was one of the lost children called Tootles?"

"Yes, he was."

"I am in a story. Hurrah, I am in a story, Nibs," chirped Tootles.

"Hush. Now I want you to think of the unhappy parents with all their children flown away," Wendy scolded.

"Oooo!" they all moaned, not really thinking of the feelings of the unhappy parents one bit.

"Think of the empty beds!"

"Oooo!"

"It's awfully sad," the first Twin said cheerfully.

"I don't see how it can have a happy ending,"

said the second Twin. "Do you, Nibs?"

"If you knew how great a mother's love is," Wendy told them proudly, "you would have no fear." She had now come to the part that Peter hated.

"You see," Wendy said, "the children knew that the mother would always leave the window open for when they flew back. So they stayed away for years and had a lovely time."

"Did they ever go back?"

"Of course," said Wendy, "and they found the window still standing open. Now they knew their mother had *always* loved them and knew they would return home to her! So up they flew to their mummy and daddy, and of course they were the happiest family that has ever been. The end."

That was the story, and it was, indeed, such a good story about a mother's love.

But there was someone who knew better, and when Wendy finished he uttered a groan.

"What is it, Peter?" Wendy cried, running to him, thinking he was ill.

"Wendy, you are wrong about mothers."

They all gathered round him. He began to speak softly the secret he had never dared to tell.

"Long ago," he said, "I thought, like you, that

my mother would always keep the window open for me, so I stayed away for moons and moons. When I flew back, the window was shut, for my mother had forgotten all about me, and there was another little boy sleeping in my bed."

I am not sure that this was true, but *Peter* thought it was true, and it scared them.

"Are you sure mothers are like that?" the children cried.

"Yes."

John and Wendy looked at one another and Michael began to cry.

"Wendy, let us go home," whispered John.

"Yes," she said, clutching them.

"Not tonight!?" asked the lost boys.

"At once," Wendy replied firmly. "Perhaps Mother has a half broken heart by this time."

Then she added rather sharply, "Peter, will you get everything set for our return?"

"If you wish it," he replied. (He was actually a bit angry, of course.) "I will request that the Indians guide you through the woods."

"Thank you, Peter."

"Then Tinker Bell will take you across the sea. Wake her, Nibs."

Of course, Tink was happy to hear that Wendy was going, but she did not want to be her guide. She said so in very naughty language. Then she pretended to be asleep again.

"She says she won't!" Nibs exclaimed.

"Tink," Peter called out, "if you don't get up and dress at once I will open the curtains, and

then we shall all see you in your nightgown."

This made her leap to the floor. "Who said I wasn't getting up?" she cried.

The boys looked sadly at Wendy.

"Dear ones," she said, "if you will all come with me, I'm sure I can get my father and mother to adopt you."

At once they jumped with joy. "Peter, can we go?" they all begged.

"All right," Peter replied with a bitter smile. They rushed to get their things.

"Get *your* things, Peter," Wendy said.

"No," he answered, pretending to be busy. "I am not going with you, Wendy."

"Yes, Peter."

"No."

"But don't you want to find your mother?" she coaxed.

"No, no," he told Wendy firmly. "Perhaps she would say I was old, and I just want to always be a little boy and to have fun."

"But, Peter—" Wendy's voice had begun to shake.

"No."

And so the others had to be told.

"Peter isn't coming."

Peter not coming! They gazed blankly at him. They carried their bundles on sticks over their backs.

"Now then," cried Peter, "no fuss, no crying. Good-bye, Wendy." He held out his hand cheerily and pretended not to care. (But of course, we know he does, don't we?)

Wendy shook his hand sadly.

"You will remember about changing your pajamas, Peter?" she said. She was always so particular about their pajamas.

"Yes."

"And you will take your medicine?"

"Yes."

There was a silence. Peter was not the kind to cry in front of others. "Are you ready, Tinker Bell?" he called out.

"Aye, aye."

"Then lead the way."

Tink darted up the nearest tree. No one followed her, for it was at this moment that the pirates made their attack upon the Indians. Above, where there had been silence, there were now the awful sounds of shrieking and the clashing of steel. All of the children froze in horror and some of the smaller ones ran to hide. As for Peter, he seized his sword!

CHAPTER FOURTEEN

The Children Are Carried Off

The pirate attack had been a complete surprise. The Piccaninnies knew that the pirates were on the island, but the Indians had fallen asleep. When they awoke, they found the pirates upon them and the battle was over very quickly. The Indians fought bravely, but were defeated by the pirates. The tribe ran into the woods to safety. Hook, however, did not stop to celebrate, for it was not the Indians he had come to destroy. It was Pan he wanted—Pan and Wendy and the boys, but mostly Pan.

Peter was such a small boy, yet Hook hated him so. Peter had flung Hook's arm to the crocodile, but, you see, there was more that Hook hated about the boy. Peter was cocky, and bold—and it was this very boldness that had gotten on Hook's nerves. It made his iron claw twitch. At night it disturbed him like an insect. More than anything, Hook wanted to be feared by all the cocky, bold, and joyous boys who would *ever* hear the name of Hook. He knew that Peter did not fear him and that the boys considered him a game. Soon enough they may all even forget Hook existed. It was this thought that drove the nasty-hearted captain crazy!

In the meantime, what of the boys? We have seen them running for hiding places and Peter getting ready for battle. But now all was quiet. Which side had won?

The pirates were listening at the hollow trees and heard every word.

"If the Injuns have won," Peter said, "they will beat the tom-tom drum. It is always their sign of victory."

Now Smee had found the tom-tom, and Hook quietly told him to beat on it. Smee smiled at the evil plan. Twice Smee beat upon the drum, and then stopped to listen gleefully.

"The tom-tom," the pirates heard Peter cry. "An Indian victory!" The poor children cheered and then went to wriggle up their trees to the ground above. The evil pirates smirked at each other and rubbed their hands together. Each pirate stood by a tree—ready to snatch the boys.

The first to emerge from his tree was Curly. He rose out of it into the arms of Cecco, who flung him to Smee, who flung him to Starkey, who flung him to Noodler, who flung him till he fell at the feet of the black pirate. All the boys were plucked from their trees in this same rude manner. Several of them were in the air at a time, like bales of hay flung from hand to hand.

Wendy, who came last, received a different treatment. She rose from her tree and Hook raised his hat to her. He offered her his arm, and escorted her to the spot where the others were being gagged. He did it with such an air. He was so frightfully polite that she forgot to cry out. She was only a little girl.

The children were tied up to keep them from flying away. All went well until Slightly's turn came. As soon as one part of him was tied up, another bit bulged out. Hook looked on as the pirates tried to tie the round little boy up. Suddenly, the evil pirate began to giggle with glee. How, he wondered, did this plump little boy go up and down a tree without getting stuck? Surely his tree must be fairly large to fit *him*!

Hook glared at Slightly, looking him up and down. Then he smiled as if he were planning something. Poor Slightly began to shudder, for he knew Hook was thinking of going down *his* hollowed-out tree. *Oh, poor Peter!* worried Slightly. *Now Hook would have him for sure.*

Hook could hardly wait to surprise the boy captain. He ordered that the captives be taken to the ship. The pirates flung the children into a huge basket and with a great "Heave Ho!" tossed the basket upon their shoulders and marched off through the forest, singing their hateful pirate chorus.

The first thing Hook did on finding himself alone was to tiptoe to Slightly's tree and make sure that he would fit inside. He listened for any sound from below, but all was silent. The house under the ground seemed to be empty and still. Was that boy asleep, or did he stand waiting at the foot of Slightly's tree, with his dagger in hand?

There was no way of knowing but by going down. He dropped his cloak to the ground and slipped into the trunk of the tree like a great black snake. He dropped silently out the other end, and stood still. As his eyes got used to the dim light he saw a great bed in the corner. A smile crept across his face, for there—fast asleep—lay Peter Pan.

* * * * * * CHAPTER FIFTEEN * * * * * *

Do You Believe in Fairies?

Peter had no idea of what happened above. He was playing joyfully on his pipes—no doubt trying to prove to himself that he did not care. Then he nearly cried—but it struck him how childish he would seem and so he laughed instead. He laughed a great bold laugh and fell asleep in the middle of it.

Thus Hook found him. He stood silent at the foot of Slightly's tree, looking across the chamber at his enemy. It was then that his eyes rested on Peter's medicine within easy reach on the ledge. He took from his coat pocket a wicked potion given to him by an evil sea witch. He always

carried it with him for he never knew when he might need it to poison an enemy. (And to Hook, there was no greater enemy than Peter Pan.) He pulled the cork from the small bottle and poured a few yellowish drops into Peter's cup.

Then he turned and wormed his way up the tree. As he climbed out at the top he looked meaner than ever. He put on his hat and pulled his cloak around him. Holding one end in front of his face to hide himself from the night, he sneaked away through the trees.

Peter slept on. It must have been not less than ten o'clock (by the crocodile) when he suddenly sat up in his bed, wakened by something. It was a soft cautious tapping on the door of his tree. Peter felt for his dagger till his hand gripped it.

"Let me in, Peter," said a lovely bell-like voice.

It was Tink, and quickly he unbarred the door. She flew in excitedly, her face flushed and her dress stained with mud.

"What is it?"

"Oh, you could never guess!" she cried, and told of the capture of Wendy and the boys.

Peter's heart bobbed up and down as he listened. Wendy tied up!—on the pirate ship!

"I'll rescue her!" he cried, leaping at his weapons. As he leapt he thought of something he could do to please Wendy. He could take his medicine. He picked up his cup.

"No!" shrieked Tinker Bell, who had heard Hook mutter about his wicked deed as he sped through the forest.

"Why not?"

"It is poisoned."

"Poisoned? Who could have poisoned it?"

"Hook."

"Don't be silly. How could Hook have got down here?"

Alas, Tinker Bell could not explain this, for even she did not know. But she did not mistake Hook's words. The cup was poisoned.

"Besides," said Peter, quite sure she was mistaken, "I never fell asleep."

He raised the cup. No time for words now—time for deeds. With one of her lightning movements, Tink got between his lips and the potion, and drank it all.

"Why, Tink, how dare you drink my medicine?"

But she did not answer. Already she was reeling in the air.

"What is the matter with you?" cried Peter, suddenly afraid.

"It was poisoned, Peter," she told him softly, "and now I am going to be dead."

"Oh, Tink, did you drink it to save me?"

"Yes."

"But why, Tink?"

Her wings would scarcely carry her now, but in reply she alighted on his shoulder and gave his chin a loving bite. She whispered in his ear, "You silly nincompoop," and then, fluttering to her chamber, lay down on the bed.

Peter's head almost filled the opening to her little room as he knelt near her in distress. Every moment her light was growing fainter, and he knew that if it went out she would be no more.

Her voice was so low, Peter could barely hear her. She was saying that she thought she could get well again if children believed in fairies.

Peter flung out his arms. There were no children there and it was night time. But he addressed all who might be dreaming of the Neverland, and who were nearer to him than you think—boys and girls in their nighties, and naked Indian babes in their baskets hung from trees.

"Do you believe?" he cried.

Tink sat up to listen to her fate.

"What do you think?" she asked Peter.

"If you believe," he shouted to them, "clap your hands! Don't let Tink die!"

Many clapped.

Some didn't.

A few beastly children hissed.

But the clapping had saved Tink! First her voice grew strong, then she popped out of bed, then she was flashing through the room more merry than ever.

"And now to rescue Wendy," proclaimed Peter.

The moon was riding in a cloudy heaven when Peter rose from his tree, armed with weapons and ready to fight. He had hoped to fly, but feared the enemy would see him. There was no other course but to press forward in Injun fashion. The crocodile passed him, but no other living thing—not a sound, not a movement. Yet he knew well that sudden death might be at the next tree, or stalking him from behind.

He swore this terrible oath: "Hook or me this time."

He was frightfully happy.

* * * * * * CHAPTER SIXTEEN * * * * * *

The Pirate Ship

One green light over Kidd's Creek marked where the pirate ship, the *Jolly Roger*, lay in the black water. Hook strolled the deck and smiled when he thought of the boys walking the plank. Ah! to be free from Peter Pan! He called roughly to his men, "Are all the children chained, so that they cannot fly away?"

"Aye, aye."

"Then hoist them up."

The poor prisoners were dragged up on deck, all except Wendy, and lined up in front of him. For a time Hook paid no attention to them. He strolled about the deck, humming in quite a lovely voice, and twirling a cigar between his fingers. His face was clouded in foul-smelling smoke. He smiled at them with all his razor-like teeth.

"Now then, bullies," he said briskly, "six of you walk the plank tonight, but I have room for two cabin boys. Which of you is it to be?"

The boys stared down at the deck nervously.

"You, boy," he said, addressing John, "you look as if you had a little pluck in you. Did you never want to be a pirate, my hearty?"

Now, John had sometimes thought of this and was surprised that Hook had picked him.

"I once thought of calling myself Red-handed Jack," he said.

"And a good name, too. We'll call you that here, bully, if you join."

"What do you think, Michael?" asked John.

"What would you call me if I join?" Michael demanded.

"Blackbeard Joe."

Michael was very impressed. "What do you think, John?" He wanted John to decide, and John wanted him to decide.

"Will we still be good subjects of the King?" John inquired.

Hook clenched his teeth. "You would have to swear *'Down with the King.'* "

John puffed out his chest. "Then I refuse," he cried, banging the barrel in front of Hook.

"And I refuse," cried Michael.

"Hooray for England! God save the King!" squeaked Curly.

The pirates covered their mouths and Hook roared out, "That seals your doom. Bring up their mother. Get the plank ready."

They were only boys, and they went white as sheets when they saw Jukes and Cecco preparing the fatal plank. But they tried to look brave when Wendy was brought up.

"So, my beauty," said Hook sweetly, "you are to see your children walk the plank."

"Are they to die?" asked Wendy, with a look of such frightful scorn that he nearly fainted.

"They are," he snarled. Then he added with a smirk, "Silence, all! for a mother's last words to her children!"

At this moment Wendy was grand. "These are my last words, dear boys," she said firmly. "I feel that I have a message to you from your real mothers, and it is this: 'We hope our sons will die like English gentlemen. God save the King!' "

Even the pirates were in awe, and the boys all cried out, "I am going to do what my mother hopes!"

"Tie her to the mast, Smee!" Hook bellowed.

The boys stood shivering and staring at the plank. Hook smiled on them with his teeth closed, and took a step toward Wendy. He wanted to turn her face so that she could see the boys walking the plank one by one. But he never reached her. A terrible sound froze him solid in his tracks.

It was the terrible *tick tick tick tick* of the crocodile!

They all heard it—the pirates, the boys, and Wendy. Immediately every head turned in one direction—not toward the water and the sound, but toward Hook.

He whimpered and fell into a little heap.

The sound came steadily nearer, and all were thinking a ghastly thought: *The crocodile is about to board the ship!*

Even the iron claw hung limp—as if knowing that it was no use against the great crocodile. Hook stayed low and crawled on his knees along the deck as far from the sound as he could go. The pirates stepped out of his way and cleared a path. It was only when Hook came up against the side of the ship that he spoke.

"Hide me!" he cried hoarsely.

The pirates gathered round him as the whimpering man crouched into a ball to make himself smaller, perhaps hoping to become invisible.

Only when Hook was hidden from them did the boys rush to the ship's side to see the crocodile climbing it. Then they got the strangest surprise of the Night of Nights. It was no crocodile that was coming to their aid. It was Peter, saying, "Tick tick tick tick..."

He signed to them not to cheer. Then he went on tick-tick-ticking.

CHAPTER SEVENTEEN

"Hook or Me This Time"

Peter had been doing such a super job of ticking that he had attracted the crocodile, who thought he was friendly because of his tick. Peter slithered into the boat, leaving the crocodile below in the water, and vanished into the cabin.

The pirates were gathering up the courage to look around.

"It's gone, Captain," Smee said, wiping off his glasses. "All is still again."

Slowly Hook raised his head and listened very hard. There was not a sound, and he drew himself up to his full height.

"Then here's to Johnny Plank!" he cried,

hating the boys more than ever because they had seen him sobbing and frightened. He broke into the pirate ditty:

"Yo ho, yo ho, the frisky plank,
You walks along it so,
Till it goes down and you goes down
To Davy Jones below!"

To scare the prisoners even more, he pretended to be dancing along a plank, leering at them as he sang. When he finished he cried, "Do you want a touch of the cat-o'-nine-tails before you walk the plank?"

At that they fell on their knees. "No, no! Not the whip!" they cried.

"Fetch the cat, Noodler," said Hook. "It's in the cabin."

The cabin! Peter was in the cabin! The children gazed at each other.

"Aye, aye," said Noodler gladly, and he went into the cabin. The boys followed him with their eyes.

Suddenly a dreadful screech came from the cabin. It wailed through the ship, and died away.

Then was heard a crowing sound. Of course, the boys knew what this meant, but to the pirates this was more eerie than the screech.

"What was that?" cried Hook.

Cecco hesitated for a moment and then swung into the cabin. He tottered out with wide, scared eyes.

"What's the matter with Bill Jukes, you dog?" hissed Hook.

"The matter with him is he's out—clunked," replied Cecco.

"Bill Jukes out!" cried the pirates.

"The cabin's as black as a pit," Cecco said, "but there is something terrible in there—the thing you heard crowing."

"Cecco," Hook said in his most steely voice, "go back and fetch me out that crowing cock-a-doodle-doo."

Cecco went, flinging his arms wildly. All listened—and again came a screech and again a crow.

" 'Sdeath and odds fish!" Hook thundered. "Who is to bring me that doodle-doo?"

No one spoke. All the pirates looked at their shoes. Hook grunted in fury. He seized a lantern,

raised his claw, and cried, "I'll bring out that doodle-doo myself," as he sped into the cabin.

Silence. Then Hook came staggering out without his lantern.

"Something blew out the light," he whispered.

"What of Cecco?" demanded Noodler.

"He's as out as Jukes," said Hook shortly.

"The ship's doomed!" cried Cookson. All of the pirates looked as if they might jump into the sea and swim for shore.

"Lads," Hook cried to his crew, "now here's a thought. Open the cabin door and drive these worthless boys in. Let *them* fight the doodle-doo for their lives!"

The boys, pretending to struggle, were pushed into the cabin and the door was closed on them.

"Now, listen!" cried Hook.

They all listened.

Meanwhile in the cabin, Peter had found the key that would free the boys of their shackles. Now they all sneaked out the back cabin door and went silently about the ship, gathering daggers and swords. Then they hid, waiting for Peter's signal.

Peter slipped out and cut Wendy's ropes.

He whispered for her to hide herself like the others. Then he took a great breath—*and crowed.*

"What's that?" cried the pirates, fearful that the awful beast had escaped the cabin and was upon them.

"Peter Pan the avenger!" came the terrible answer. As he spoke, Peter jumped out. Then they all knew who it was that had been in the cabin. Twice Hook tried to speak and twice he failed. In that frightful moment I think his fierce heart broke.

At last he cried, "At him, my hearties!"

"Down, boys, and at them!" Peter's voice rang out.

In another moment the clash of knives and daggers and swords sounded through the ship. The frightened pirates were not prepared for such bravery from the boys. To escape, the villains started leaping into the sea. Some hid in dark corners and closets. Slightly found them in their hiding places, and drove them out by flashing a lantern in their eyes. It was a grand fight! The pirates were clearly losing, for they all had to escape to the sea—one by one. All but Hook, that is.

I think all were gone when a group of savage boys surrounded Hook. Again and again they closed upon him, and again and again he swung his great hook at them. Just then another sprang into the middle.

"Put away your swords, boys," cried the newcomer. "This man is mine."

Thus suddenly Hook found himself face to face with Peter. The others drew back and formed a ring around them.

For a long time the two enemies looked at

one another. Hook shuddered slightly, and Peter stood with a strange smile upon his face.

"So, Pan," said Hook at last, "this is all your doing."

"Aye, James Hook," came the stern answer, "it is all my doing."

"Bold and cocky boy," said Hook, "prepare to meet thy doom."

"Dark and sinister man," Peter answered, "have at thee."

Without more words, they fell to sword fighting. Hook fought with great skill and it seemed that every sweep of that terrible sword would have done in the boy. Peter just fluttered round him and leapt from danger each time. Again and again the boy darted in and nicked his dark enemy. Hook sawed the air with his claw, trying to spear the boy. Peter crouched under it and jabbed Hook in the ribs. At the sight of his own blood—whose strange color, you remember, made him ill—Hook dropped his sword and was at the mercy of the brave boy.

"Pan, who and what art thou?" he cried hoarsely.

"I'm youth, I'm joy," Peter answered joyously, "I'm a little bird that has broken out of the egg."

"And I," snarled Hook, "shall be known forever as the one who defeated this youth—this joy! The name of Hook will spark fear in the hearts of all children! My time is at hand!"

(James Hook, farewell. For we have come to his last moment.)

Leaving the fight, Hook rushed into the gunpowder room and lit a fuse to an explosive shell. He ran back out crying, "In two minutes the ship will be blown to pieces!" He sprang upon the side of the ship to jump to safety in the sea. (He did not know that the crocodile was waiting, for the clock's tick had run down.)

Peter rushed into the gunpowder room—

"To shore! Farewell!" cried Hook.

—and came out with the lit shell in his hands—

The wicked pirate waved his claw—

—and then Peter calmly flung the shell overboard.

—then Hook calmly flung himself overboard—and into the waiting jaws of the crocodile.

Thus ended James Hook.

Wendy, of course, had stood by, taking no part in the fight. Now that the battle was over, she again took the lead. She praised all the brave boys equally. Then she took them into Hook's

cabin and pointed to his watch that was hanging on a nail. It said "half-past one"! They were up well past their bedtime! Imagine!

Wendy got them to bed in the pirates' bunks pretty quickly, you may be sure—all but Peter, who had dressed himself up as a pirate. He strutted up and down on the deck, until at last he fell asleep by the side of Long Tom.

* * * * * CHAPTER EIGHTEEN * * * * *

The Return Home

Of course, by and by the three naughty children and their shipmates (all had dressed up as nasty pirates by now, of course) made it home to Number 14. There in the nursery, with broken hearts, sat the Darlings and Nana. Mrs. Darling had indeed kept the window open, and when the three children saw it, their hearts leapt with joy. They flew in and landed softly on the floor.

"John," said Michael, looking around. "I think I have been here before."

"Of course you have, you silly. There is your old bed."

"So it is," Michael said, wondering.

It was then that Wendy saw a figure in the next room.

"It's Mother!" cried Wendy, peeping.

"So it is!" said John.

"Then, are you not really our mother, Wendy?" asked Michael, who was surely sleepy.

"Oh, dear!" exclaimed Wendy. "It was quite time we came back."

They ran into the next room with shouts of gleeful homecoming.

"Mother!" Wendy cried.

"Here's Wendy!" said Mrs. Darling with surprise. She was sure it was a dream.

"Mother!"

"And John!" Mother cried.

"Mother!" cried Michael. He knew her now.

"And here is Michael!" she exclaimed, weeping. She stretched out her arms for the three little selfish children who had run to her.

"George, George!" she called when she could speak.

Mr. Darling ran in.

Nana came rushing in.

There could not have been a lovelier, happier sight—but there was no one to see it except a little boy who was staring in at the window. He had lived countless joys and many wonderful adventures that other children can never know—but none could measure having the love of a mother and father.

I hope you want to know what became of the other boys. They were waiting below to give Wendy time to explain about them. When they had counted to five hundred, they went up. (They went up by the stair, because they thought this would make a better impression.) They stood in a row in front of Mrs. Darling, with their hats off, wishing they were not wearing their pirate clothes. They said nothing, but their eyes asked her to keep them. Of course Mrs. Darling said at once that she would have them, and Mr. Darling, scratching his head at the number of them, finally agreed.

As for Peter, he saw Wendy once again before he flew away. He did not exactly come to the window, but he brushed against it in passing so that she could open it if she liked and call to him. That is what she did.

"Hullo, Wendy, good-bye," he said.

"Oh, dear! Are you going away?"

"Yes."

"Will you come again and visit us?" Wendy asked hopefully.

"Well, I am awfully busy you know, being a captain and all. But I suppose I can visit sometimes," Peter replied with a mischievous smile. "After all, I cannot let you forget how to fly."

And with a wink and a giggle, he leapt from the windowsill into the night air and was gone.

Oh, but don't worry. Peter did return to the nursery—and the children had many more smashing adventures and games. For you see, Peter will always be found where there are children who seek adventure and fun in the land of make-believe...

And so it will always go as long as children are young and bright...

... and believe.

THE END

ABOUT THE AUTHOR

J. M. BARRIE

In 1860, James Matthew Barrie was born into poverty in a village in Scotland. His father, a handloom weaver, and mother had ten children. James was the ninth. The hope of the family was James's smart older brother, David. When David was killed in a skating accident, James vowed to take his place and make a fortune for the family. He studied hard and went on to Edinburgh University. He became a successful journalist and writer. His humorous and well-written stories became popular throughout Scotland and England—and, later, around the world.

In his thirties, Barrie became a playwright, married an actress, and met a family that would change his life—the Davieses and their five sons. Barrie created tales about lost boys and Peter Pan to amuse the Davies children. Together they played Indians and pirates. Their adventures were turned into a play called *Peter Pan* that became wildly successful. In 1911, the story was written into book form.

Barrie was made a baronet and became Sir James Barrie. He died in 1937 and left the copyright to his famous story to a London hospital for sick children.